*P*ROVENCE
*C*OOKING

WRITTEN BY
ÉLISABETH BOURGEOIS

PHOTOGRAPHY
PIERRE MANETTI

SOMMELIER
PHILIPPE BAIQUE

BARNES
&NOBLE
BOOKS
NEW YORK

*To my daughter Emmanuelle
and my grand-daughter Chiara*

Creative direction : Hervé Amiard

CONTENTS

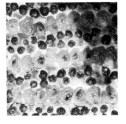

Simple Pleasures

« *W*hen I was seven years old, my father gave me a pretty little Louis XIII bench that he had bought while indulging his passion for auction sales. Standing on the bench, I could reach the table and marvel at my mother's culinary genius. It wasn't easy for such a small child, but I soon learned how to knead pie crust, place it carefully into the prepared quiche pan and garnish it with quarters of wrinkled apples from our garden. That was in 1955 in our family restaurant, 'Le Gai Logis' in Champagny-sur-Yonne in France.

For my mother, cooking was a labor of love. She was an excellent cook who would delight her customers (who soon became friends) with simple but delicious fare such as pike or carp fresh from the local pond and vegetables lovingly tended by my grandfather Léon in his precious vegetable patch. The kitchen walls gleamed with rows of copper saucepans inherited from my grandmother, a woman of imposing stature who for 50 years had held the fort in a tiny restaurant called 'Aux Marches des Flandres' (On the Steps of Flanders).

My mother soon entrusted me with small tasks that I would proudly fulfil and I rapidly became more adventurous. Together with my sister Maryse, who was 18 months my senior, I would take advantage of my parents' rare absences to try my hand at other culinary exploits aided and abetted by grandfather Bourgeois who had a healthy appetite and was only too happy to serve as our guinea pig.

It did not take my parents long to realize that whereas I was a hopeless scholar, I did seem to have a gift for cooking. For my part, I was itching to start work: it was decided that I should become a cook.

My family is not originally from Provence but from Paris where I was born. My parents, who made their living out of food and cooking, travelled in the line of business which is how we came to move to the south of France in the winter of 1962, first to the lovely village of Jouques, very near Aix-en-Provence, then to Cavaillon where my family opened the 'Miradou'. I spent the next few years 'apprenticed' to my mother, learning her exacting craft.

Within a very few years, I was married and had given birth to our daughter Emmanuelle. My love of cooking blossomed encouraged by 'regulars' such as the Provençal writer Marie Mauron who taught me the difference between so-called traditional cooking and the real thing. *La Cuisinière Provençale* (The Provençale Cook) by Reboul became my bible. Then I struck up a friendship with Jean Chaudat, a remarkably gifted young chef who in his tragically short lifetime managed to turn an instinctive talent into an art. When I was 24 years old, I opened the 'Petit Bedon' ('The Little Paunch') my first restaurant in Avignon. Inspired by Michel Guérard's cuisine nouvelle, sauces became lighter, salads became wilder and for the next eight years the restaurant featured in all the major guidebooks. By that time, I felt confident enough to take on the job of head cook at the 'Mas de la Bertrande' where I stayed for the next five years.

After that, Philippe and I longed for a house of our own and a return to our first love, the Lubéron. We bought the 'Mas de Tourteron', a former silkworm nursery nestling between the vineyards and the olive groves at the foot of the pretty village of Gordes. From the village, a winding road leads to a path bordered with white flowers and a walled garden with a heavy wooden gate that opens onto a magical place shaded by an ancient lime tree. The house itself is tall and very handsome and dates from around 1850. It became our home and workplace as Philippe and I gradually organized our daily lives around its rhythm, waking every morning to a garden in brilliant shades of white and blue, my favorite color. There is a huge kitchen that opens onto the garden, exactly like a traditional country kitchen with rows of polished saucepans that I inherited from my mother, spice pots and a glazed frieze. To our customers who are mostly all friends, it is a haven of peace and a chance to gather around a table fragrant with the scents of Provence.

My aim in writing this book is to recreate some of the magic of our daily life at the 'Mas Tourteron' where every occasion – whether a celebration, picnic or gathering of friends – revolves around a kitchen of simple pleasures.   E. B.

STARTERS

$\mathcal{M}$Y CHILLED PLUM TOMATO SOUP

*Method: easy   Preparation time: 20 min
Cooking time: 5 min the day before*

– ❋ –

Serves 6

**8 medium sized plum
tomatoes**

**2 tablespoons balsamic
vinegar**

**3 3/4 tablespoons tapenade
(olive paste - see p. 109)**

**2 slices from a white
sandwich loaf**

1 dash Tabasco

1/2 cup olive oil

**1/2 teaspoon salt
and pepper**

4 *cébettes*

1 shallot (minced)

2 garlic cloves (minced)

croutons to garnish

– ❋ –

Soak the tomatoes in boiling water for two min, peel and crush. Heat the olive oil with the garlic and shallots, add the tomatoes and cook for five min. Purée in a vegetable mill (on the finest setting), add the vinegar, Tabasco, salt, pepper and sugar. Leave to chill overnight.
Cut the bread into little cubes, fry until golden and spread with *tapenade*. Snip the *cébettes*. Serve garnished with the croutons and sprinkled with the snipped *cébettes*.

Cébettes are vegetables similar to the leek with a crisp green stalk that I snip into summer salads and sprinkle over chilled soups. Make sure you choose plump, ripe tomatoes that give this soup a lovely red color.

SERVE WITH:
A crisp, fresh white wine.

$\mathcal{M}$Y MELON SOUP APPETIZER

Method: very easy   Preparation time: 5 min

- ✸ -

Serves 6

4 heavy melons

3 tablespoons Pastis

6 crushed ice cubes

Salt and pepper

Wild fennel

- ✸ -

Peel the three melons and scoop out all the seeds. Process in the blender with the Pastis and the crushed ice cubes, season and set aside to chill.

Open the fourth melon, remove the seeds and using a vegetable ball cutter, scoop the center of the melon into balls.

Serve the soup in pretty goblets, garnished with the melon balls. I like to decorate with tips of wild fennel that you find growing along the footpaths in Provence – I call them 'little umbrellas'.

$\mathcal{M}$Y SUMMER ARUGULA SOUP

Method: quite easy   Preparation time: 15 min
Cooking time: 5 min

- ✸ -

Serves 4

Good pound washed arugula leaves

Bare 1/2 cup olive oil

Bare 1/2 cup poultry broth

1 teaspoon balsamic vinegar

Salt and pepper

1/2 cup Parmesan shavings

A few small croutons fried in olive oil

1 tablespoon crème fraîche or a few crushed ice cubes

- ✸ -

Blanche half the arugula by plunging in boiling salted water. Drain well and pat dry with a tea towel.

Place the olive oil in the blender, followed by the raw arugula, bell pepper and blanched arugula. Gradually add the warm poultry broth and blend until you obtain a fine purée. Chill.

Pour into the soup tureen, adding the balsamic vinegar and salt. Decorate with Parmesan shavings and small fried croutons.

This soup may be served chilled on top of one two crushed ice cubes or warm with a tablespoon of crème fraîche.

Arugula is a Mediterranean lettuce with quite a strong peppery, bitter taste. Choose only the smallest, smoothest leaves.

$\mathcal{C}$HILLED GARDEN HERB MOUSSES

Method: easy   Preparation time: 15 min
Cooking time: 25 min

– ✻ –

Serves 6

3 green bell peppers

3 red bell peppers

3 yellow bell peppers

2 ribs celery

2 envelopes gelatin

4 sprigs tarragon

1 clove garlic

1 cup light crème fraîche

A few drops Tabasco

Olive oil

Salt and pepper

– ✻ –

Soften the gelatin in a little cold water.

Toast the bell peppers in the oven for 20 min, skin and cut into strips keeping the colors separate. Peel, core and chop the garlic. Cut the celery ribs into tiny dice.

Warm the olive oil slightly in three separate saucepans. Add one type of bell pepper to each saucepan along with the diced celery, garlic, tarragon, salt and pepper. Leave to simmer for a few min. Share the gelatin between the three saucepans, stir well and leave to dissolve. Add the Tabasco. When cool, mix to obtain three smooth purées.

Beat the cream and add even amounts to each purée, stirring carefully.

Line the inside of a bowl with plastic wrap leaving a wide overhanging border. Line with the peeled tomato quarters, then fill with the garden herb mousse and cover tightly with the plastic wrap. Chill and turn out before serving.

These mousses may also be made with eggplants or tomatoes. I like to serve them with olive bread or fougassette (crusty lattice-like bread made of sweet dough, often flavored with anchovies, black olives, herbs, spices or onions).

$\mathcal{B}$ELL PEPPER AND *CÉBETTE* SALAD

Method: very easy   Preparation time: 15 min
Cooking time: 15 min

– * –

Serves 6

2 green bell peppers

2 red bell peppers

2 yellow bell peppers

4 tomatoes

4 young cébettes

1/4 cup lemon juice

1/4 cup olive oil

1 teaspoon coriander seeds

1/2 teaspoon ground

coriander

1/2 small chili

1 tablespoon cumin powder

Salt and pepper

– * –

Scorch the bell peppers on a naked flame and remove the skins by wrapping in newspaper or a plastic bag (but do not soak). Remove the seeds and cut into strips. Plunge the tomatoes into boiling water, then peel and cut into small cubes.

Heat the olive oil, add the garlic followed by the spices and finally the lemon. Add the tomatoes, bell peppers and finely snipped cébettes. Season. Cook for 15 min over a low flame. Serve chilled.

$\mathcal{L}$ITTLE CUCUMBER CANAPÉS
WITH CREAMED GARBANZOS

Method: quite easy   Preparation time: 20 min the day before
Cooking time: 1 hour 30 min

— ❋ —

Serves 6

2 firm cucumbers

6 anchovies in oil

1 1/4 cups garbanzos

2/3 cup olive oil

2 cored garlic cloves

1 onion stuck with a clove

For the court bouillon:

1 bay leaf

2 carrots

1 rib celery

Peel of one orange

— ❋ —

Prepare the court bouillon, cook for 10 min and leave to cool. Meanwhile, halve the cucumbers lengthwise and scoop out the seeds with a teaspoon. Using a small biscuit cutter, cut out little tartlet shapes in the two halves of the cucumber. Plunge the garbanzos into the cooled court bouillon, bring to a boil, skim and leave to cook gently for 1 hour 30 min. Drain the chickpeas well.

Pour the garbanzos into the blender, drizzle in the olive oil and add the garlic, salt and pepper.

Place the creamed garbanzos into a decorating bag, pipe onto the cucumber tartlets and chill.

These little chickpea canapés are ideal with drinks.

$\mathcal{L}$ITTLE POTS OF FARMER'S CHEESE WITH GRATED CUCUMBER

Method: very easy   Preparation time: 5 min
No cooking required

— ✻ —

Serves 6

2 cups smooth cream cheese

or goat's cheese

2 cucumbers

Handful golden raisins

1 tablespoon cumin powder

1/2 tablespoon cinnamon

powder

Pinch curry powder

1 finely snipped shallot

1 tablespoon lemon juice

Fresh mint leaves

to decorate

Salt and pepper

— ✻ —

Peel and grate the cucumbers like carrots and mix with the cream cheese. Add the spices, golden raisins, finely snipped shallots, lemon juice. Season and chill.

Decorate with mint leaves and serve with toast.

SERVE WITH:
A fairly sharp white vin de pays.

$\mathcal{L}$ITTLE GOAT'S CHEESES ROASTED WITH ROSEMARY

*Method: very easy   Preparation time: 10 min
Cooking time: 10 min*

— ✳ —

Serves 6

**6 small, fairly moist
goat's cheeses**

3 tomatoes

6 sprigs fresh rosemary

Drizzle of olive oil

**Salt and freshly
milled pepper**

6 small casserole dishes

— ✳ —

Plunge the tomatoes in boiling water for 2 min, cool and peel. Chop into small cubes and spoon into the base of the small casserole dishes. Place one goat's cheese into each dish, season, add a sprig of rosemary and drizzle with olive oil. Oven-broil for 10 min.

These are best made with deliciously creamy 'Picodon' goat's cheeses from the Valréas area of France. With their thin rind and nutty flavor they are particularly well suited to this recipe.

$\mathcal{E}$GGPLANT AND TOMATO FRITTERS

Method: easy   Preparation time: 5 min
Cooking time: 2 min

— ✳ —

Serves 6-8

2 thinly sliced eggplants

4 plum tomatoes

8 preserved tomato halves

1 cup batter (see p. 109)

Handful sage leaves

Salt and pepper

— ✳ —

Place half a preserved tomato (or a slice of fresh tomato) between two slices of eggplant and add a sage leaf. Dip into the batter and fry carefully for 3 min. Drain well on paper towels. Season.

$\mathcal{Z}$UCCHINI AND ANCHOVY FRITTERS

— ✳ —

Serves 6-8

11 ounces fresh anchovies, filleted and washed

2 zucchini cut into thin round slices

1 cup batter (see p. 109)

— ✳ —

Method: easy   Preparation time: 5 min
Cooking time: 5 min

Place one well-drained anchovy fillet between two round slices of zucchini. Dip into the batter and fry carefully for 2 min. Drain well on paper towels. Serve with drinks and a bowl of *anchoïade* (see p. 109).

𝒯ABOULEH

*Method: easy   Preparation time: 30 min
Cooking time: 30 min*

- ✳ -

Serves 6

**1 packet spelt or cracked
wheat(1 lb. or 2 cups)**

2 red bell peppers

2 green bell peppers

2 onions

Generous 1 1/2 cups broth

3 tomatoes

1 large bunch mint

1 1/2 cups olive oil

1 1/4 cups lemon juice

- ✳ -

Rinse the spelt wheat (or if not available, cracked wheat) in running water for 10 min then cook with the bouillon cube for a further 30 min. Rinse and leave to drain.

Meanwhile, cut the vegetables into tiny cubes and snip the mint as finely as possible.

Place the wheat in a large salad platter then add the lemon juice, olive oil, finely snipped mint and cubed vegetables. Season, mix well and chill.

German or spelt wheat is a highly nutritious species of hardy wheat that grows on impoverished soils and cooks the same way as rice. While much less cultivated than it was, it features increasingly in today's diet. Where I live, it is cultivated mainly in the foothills of the Mont Ventoux and on the Albion plateau by farmers who changed to cultivating German wheat when crisis loomed in the sheep farming industry.

SERVE WITH:
A white *Coteaux de Pierrevert from the Alpes of Haute-Provence.*

$\mathcal{G}$ LOBE ARTICHOKES WITH SALT COD BRANDADE

*Method: easy   Preparation time: 15 min
Cooking time: 10 min
Makes 12 little artichokes*

— ✳ —

Serves 6

1 lemon

2 tablespoons olive oil

Salt and pepper

1 1/3 cups salt cod *brandade*

(see p. 109)

— ✳ —

Heat a good 3 quarts of water in a kettle with the olive oil, salt, pepper and half the lemon. Wash the artichokes, cut the tips off each leaf, remove the tough outer leaves and 'choke' and sprinkle with lemon juice. Cook in the kettle for 10–12 min, then drain. When cool, stuff the artichokes with the *brandade* and sprinkle with herbs.

SERVE WITH:
Tavel, known locally as the 'Côtes du Rhone rosé'.

ONION PIZZA WITH ANCHOVIES AND BLACK OLIVES

*Method: easy   Preparation time: 20 min
Cooking time: 35 min*

— ✴ —

Serves 8

2 lb. 3 oz onions

1 quantity bread dough

made with olive oil

Olive oil

4 ounces anchovy fillets

Black olives

Olive oil

Salt and pepper

— ✴ —

Peel and fry the shredded onions in a little olive oil over a low heat until golden and slightly sticky. Place the dough in the center of a quiche pan and press out to form a lining about a 1/4 inch thick.

Prick the dough and spread with the onions. Garnish with a lattice of anchovies and sprinkle with olives. Drizzle with olive oil, season and cook for 20 min at 350°F. Serve warm.

— ✴ —

Serves 8

2 plump carrots

10 sprigs cilantro

For the batter:

3 whole eggs

1 1/3 cups all-purpose flour

1 1/3 cups milk

1 tablespoon sunflower oil

1/2 package yeast

salt and pepper

— ✴ —

LITTLE CARROT CRÊPES

*Method: very easy   Preparation time: 5 min
Cooking time: 5 min*

Peel and grate the carrots. Make the batter for the crêpes from the ingredients listed then add the carrots and sprigs of cilantro. Ladle small amounts of batter into an oiled pan and cook each pancake for a few moments per side. Drain on a piece of kitchen towel and serve warm.

*F*IVE OMELET CAKE

Method: quite hard   Preparation time: 35 min the day before
Cooking time: 1 hour for all the omelets

- ✳ -

Serves 6-8

19 eggs

2 large tomatoes

3 green and red bell peppers

11 oz cultivated mushrooms

1 bowl leftover ratatouille

Slab of country ham

(5 ounces)

2 oz mozzarella

1/2 cup unsalted butter

(1 stick)

1 clove garlic

1 shallot

1 bunch parsley and basil

Olive oil

Pinch of sugar

1 lemon

salt and pepper

1 terrine dish or

deep cake pan

with sloping sides

- ✳ -

This is a *crespéou*: a layered Provençale omelet cake with five different fillings.

Fillings:

Tomatoes: peel and crush then fry in a tablespoon of olive oil with 2 cloves of minced garlic, 1 chopped shallot, the finely snipped basil, salt, pepper and a pinch of sugar. **Bell peppers:** oven-broil, sprinkle with lemon, shred and fry with a clove of garlic, chopped parsley, salt and pepper. **Mushrooms:** wash, sprinkle with lemon, shred and fry with a clove of garlic, chopped parsley, salt and pepper. **Ratatouille:** re-heat with no extra oil. Ham and mozzarella: slice both ingredients.

Making up:

Make an omelet with 3 eggs, fry in the butter and as soon as it starts to set, spread with the tomatoes. When the omelet is cooked but moist, lift out onto a plate. Make the four other omelets in the same way, each with a different filling. Next, oil a terrine dish or deep cake pan with sloping sides.

Fill first with the tomato omelet then the four other omelets. Pour over 4 beaten eggs and sprinkle with chopped parsley. Cover the terrine, place in a roasting pan containing about 4-5 inches of boiling water and oven cook for 10 min at 350° F. When cool, weight down and leave overnight in the refrigerator.

Turn out and serve with a delicious *concassé* of tomatoes and fresh basil (see p. 108).

(see p. 108).

*S*ERVE WITH:
A lively, fresh white Côtes du Ventoux or Château Blanc.

$\mathcal{E}$GG SURPRISE APPETIZERS

Method: quite hard   Preparation time: 15-20 min
Cooking time: 5 min

– ✴ –

Serves 6

6 eggs

1 tub salmon taramasalata

1 small jar salmon eggs

1/2 red bell pepper

1/2 green bell pepper

1 clove garlic

Court bouillon made with

1 aromatic bouillon cube

Olive oil

Few sprigs dill

Salt and pepper

2/3 envelope gelatin

– ✴ –

Start by emptying the eggs: using an egg-cutter, slice off the top of the egg, empty the contents then rinse and dry the shell.

Dice the two different colored bell pepper halves and fry in a skillet for 1 min with a drizzle of olive oil and the minced garlic. Set aside.

Soften the gelatin in a little cold water then stir into the lightly warmed court bouillon. Check for seasoning and stir again.

Place the eggshells in the eggcups and fill each one with a teaspoon of the bell pepper mixture followed by enough court bouillon to cover. Leave to chill for 1 hour.

Fill a decorating bag with taramasalata and pipe over the eggs. Decorate with salmon eggs and sprigs of dill.

If the budget can stand it, why not replace the taramasalata with a teaspoon of the finest caviar?

SERVE WITH:
A young, pleasantly fruity red Côtes du Rhône.

SCRAMBLED EGGS WITH TRUFFLES

*Method: very easy   Preparation time: 5 min the day before
Cooking time: 10-12 min*

— ✳ —

Serves 4

**1 truffle weighing 2 ounces
(or more)**

10 eggs

Knob of unsalted butter

**1 tablespoon heavy
crème fraîche**

Salt and pepper

— ✳ —

The day before, scrub the truffle under the tap with a small vegetable brush to remove any dirt. Place it with the eggs in a good-size jar and seal hermetically. The eggs will become impregnated with the scent of the truffle.

When you are ready to start cooking, place a knob of butter in a double boiler. Beat the eggs in a bowl and grate the truffle setting aside four slices. Season lightly. Pour the beaten eggs into the double boiler, stirring constantly with a wooden spoon until the mixture starts to thicken. Add the crème fraîche and stir once again. Decorate with a slice of truffle and serve immediately. These scrambled eggs cannot wait.

SERVE WITH:
A strong, elegant white Hermitage.

VEGETABLES

PYRAMID OF ASPARAGUS
WITH A BROKEN EGG

*Method: the eggs require careful cooking   Preparation time: 20 min
Cooking time: 20-30 min*

‒ ✳ ‒

Serves 6

**2 firm bunches of green
asparagus**

6 cooled soft-boiled eggs

**Good 1/2 cup fine
breadcrumbs**

**2 1/2 tablespoons melted
unsalted butter**

1 deep fat fryer

Few sprigs of tarragon

‒ ✳ ‒

Peel, wash and dry the asparagus then tie in a bunch so that the stalks are even. Heat a kettle of water adding a generous pinch of salt (2 teaspoons per quart water). When the water starts to boil, plunge in the asparagus and cook for 20 to 30 min depending on the thickness of the stalks. Refresh under the cold tap and drain on a tea towel.

Meanwhile, soft boil the eggs for 5 min, leave to cool then carefully peel away the shells.

Heat the oil in the fryer, brush the eggs with melted butter then roll them in the breadcrumbs and deep fry immediately for 2 min. Drain on kitchen paper.

Arrange the asparagus on individual plates, place one soft-boiled egg on top and decorate with finely snipped tarragon.

The asparagus are eaten dipped in the soft boiled egg.

SERVE WITH:
A refreshing Muscat d'Alsace.

$\mathcal{T}$ERRINE OF GLAZED BELL PEPPERS AND FARMER'S GOAT CHEESE FLAVORED WITH LEMON BALM AND CITRONELLA

Method: quite hard   Preparation time: 30 min

— ✳ —

Serves 8-10

2 lb. 3 oz farmer's goat's cheese (loose)

3 different colored bell peppers

3/4 cup pitted, loosely minced black olives

mixed with

2 tablespoons pine nuts

2 +1/3 envelopes gelatin softened in cold water and dissolved in

1/4 cup light cream

6 zucchini

1 1/4 cups olive oil

2 garlic cloves (minced)

1 small bunch finely snipped lemon balm

1 teaspoon cumin

Salt and freshly ground pepper

Juice 1 lemon

1 large terrine dish

— ✳ —

First toast and peel the bell peppers: oven-broil, turning during cooking and, when the skin is quite black, wrap in newspaper for 15 min then remove the skins under the tap. Cut into thin slivers.

In a small saucepan, gently heat 2 tablespoons of olive oil then add the garlic, sliced bell peppers and a pinch of cumin. Season and add a pinch of finely snipped lemon balm. Stew over a low heat for 15 min and when cool, set aside to chill.

Wash the zucchini but do not peel. Slice thinly using a potato peeler then steam for 5 min. Now sprinkle with olive oil, cumin, salt and pepper and set aside covered with plastic wrap.

In a mixing bowl, mix the cheese with the minced olives and pine nuts. Add the cream mixed with the dissolved gelatin. Season lightly and set aside to chill.

Oil a terrine dish and line with the sliced zucchini. Spread a layer of the cream mixture over the base, followed by a layer of bell peppers, another layer of cream and finally slices of zucchini. Cover with plastic wrap, press down with a 2 lb. weight and chill for 24 hours.

Serve individual slices of terrine on a plate garnished with bell peppers drizzled with lemon juice. Decorate with lemon balm and citronella.

If you cannot find farmer's goat's cheese, a soft sheep's cheese or any well-drained farmer's cheese will do equally well. You can also replace the lemon balm with fresh mint

SERVE WITH:
A dry, fruity tasting Côtes du Ventoux rosé.

VEGETABLE CARPACCIO

Method: quite easy   Preparation time: 30 min
Cooking time: 15 min

– ✳ –

Serves 6

3 slim zucchini

3 long eggplants

3 red bell peppers

3 green bell peppers

6 preserved tomatoes

1 bunch fresh basil

(finely snipped)

1 bunch cilantro

plus coriander seeds

1 head garlic

1 cup olive oil

Juice of 3 lemons

Salt and pepper

Parmesan shavings

– ✳ –

Start by scorching the bell peppers on a naked flame to remove the skin, then set aside. Cut each eggplant lengthwise into six thin slices. Fry in a skillet with olive oil until golden and set aside. Season. Cut each zucchini lengthwise into six slices.

Marinade the vegetable slices as follows:

Zucchini: lay the sliced zucchini in a soup dish with a few spoonfuls of olive oil. Add salt, pepper, lemon juice, ground coriander seeds, cilantro leaves and 3 minced garlic cloves. Set aside to chill.

Eggplant: lay the sliced eggplant in a soup dish. Season and add two chopped garlic cloves plus the basil.

Bell peppers: halve the peppers lengthwise and sprinkle with olive oil and lemon juice. Add the coriander seeds, three shredded garlic cloves, chili, salt and pepper.

Arrange in a bouquet on an attractive dish, add the preserved tomatoes, sprinkle with Parmesan shavings and set aside to chill.

Preserved tomatoes, available from most Italian grocery stores, are dried tomatoes that have been preserved in a jar filled with olive oil.

$\mathcal{M}$AMMY MARCELLE'S EGGPLANT AND BACON HASH

Method: easy   Preparation time: 10 min
Cooking time: 20 min

– ✳ –

Serves 8-10

6 eggplants

1/2 cup olive oil

6 thin slices smoked bacon

6 garlic cloves,

cored and chopped

***Concassé* of tomatoes**

(see p. 108)

1 sprig thyme (chopped)

Salt and pepper

– ✳ –

Wash and dry the eggplants, dice and set aside. Slice the smoked bacon into thin matchsticks.

Heat the olive oil in a large skillet then add the bacon, eggplant, garlic, chopped thyme and seasoning. Stir and cover until the hash is a lovely golden color. Now add the *concassé* of tomatoes and leave to stew over a low heat.

This slow-cooked hash is equally delicious hot or cold, wrapped in an omelet or cooked in a pie shell made with olive oil, baked golden brown in the oven and sprinkled with Parmesan.

SERVE WITH:
The author's favorite wine: a beautifully balanced, rounded white from Saint-Bris-le-Vineux.

*F*ARANDOLE OF BABY STUFFED VEGETABLES WITH A MELODY OF FRAGRANT HERBS

*Method: quite hard   Preparation time: 1 hour
Cooking time: 20 min*

— ❋ —

Serves 6

6 small round zucchini

1 long zucchini

6 baby plum tomatoes

4 regular tomatoes

6 baby eggplants

6 new season's onions

1 large onion

1 large bell pepper

1 cup farmer's cheese

8 eggs

1 1/4 cups leftover meat

2 anchovies

1 tablespoon pine nuts

1 head garlic

4 sprigs basil

2 sprigs parsley

1 sprig oregano

1 tablespoon breadcrumbs

Vinegar

1 tablespoon grenadine

Olive oil

Salt and pepper

— ❋ —

Prepare the baby vegetables by cutting off the tops and scooping out the flesh to be used for stuffing. Set aside together with the lids. Place the emptied vegetables on a cookie sheet, season, drizzle with olive oil and cook for 5 min at 350-375°F. Now make the stuffing.

Zucchini: dice the flesh of all the zucchini and mix with the soft goat or sheep's cheese, 2 eggs, 1 garlic clove, two chopped basil stalks and the toasted and chopped pine nuts. Season.

Tomatoes: dice the flesh of the six baby tomatoes and two normal size tomatoes. Mix with the leftover meat, 2 eggs, 1 garlic clove, chopped parsley and breadcrumbs.

Eggplants: dice the flesh and mix with the flesh of two tomatoes, 2 eggs, the chopped anchovies and finely snipped basil.

Onion: chop, drizzle with vinegar, add the grenadine and cook gently for 10 min until soft and sticky.

Bell peppers: dice the flesh of all the peppers and mix with 2 eggs, 1 chopped garlic clove, 1 sprig of finely snipped oregano, salt and pepper.

Reduce each stuffing then spoon into the appropriate baby vegetables. Arrange on a cookie sheet, cover with the lids and drizzle with olive oil. Cover with tin foil and cook for 20 min at 350-375°F.

SERVE WITH:
An elegant, distinguished red Saint-Joseph.

S AUTÉED POTATOES WITH ONIONS

*Method: very easy   Preparation time: 10 min
Cooking time: 35 min*

– ✱ –

Serves 6

**3 lb. 4 oz Round White
or Round Red potatoes**

3 tablespoons goose fat

3 onions (shredded)

1 bunch chervil

Salt and pepper

– ✱ –

Peel and slice the potatoes. Heat the goose fat in a cast iron cas-serole dish and fry the potatoes until a lovely golden color. Cover and simmer for 20 min stirring from time to time. Adjust the seasoning then remove from the heat and leave to sweat.

Shred the onion then add to the potatoes and return to the heat to brown for a further 10-15 min. Season.

Serve in the casserole dish sprinkled with chervil.

In country areas, this very simple dish is traditionally served with poultry for Sunday lunch.

SERVE WITH:
A Cornas wine.

SPICY VEGETABLE GRATIN

Method: easy   Preparation time: 10 min
Cooking time: 25 min

— ✳ —

Serves 8-10

8 plump zucchini

8 small, firm tomatoes

6 eggs mixed with

6 tablespoons crème fraîche

2-3 tablespoons

unsalted butter

2 cored garlic cloves

1 bunch fresh thyme

1 pinch curry powder

1 pinch grated nutmeg

Salt and pepper

1 large oven-proof dish

— ✳ —

Wash and dry the zucchini and cut into thin, round slices. Peel and slice the tomatoes. Chop the garlic cloves, butter an oven-proof dish and rub all over with the garlic.

Beat the eggs in a mixing bowl with the spices, shredded thyme and the remaining chopped garlic. Season.

Fill the dish with rows of overlapping vegetable slices, starting with a row of zucchini followed by a row of tomatoes until there are no more vegetables left. Pre-cook the vegetables for 5 min at 400°F.

Remove from the oven, pour over the cream and egg mixture and bake again for 20 min.

This delicious gratin is usually served with a tian d'agneau *(lamb quiche).*

SERVE WITH:
A light, refreshing Loire rosé.

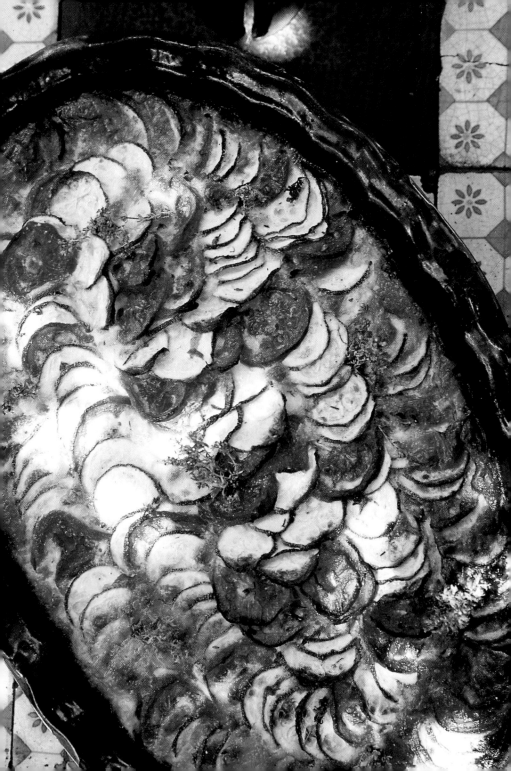

$\mathcal{Z}$UCCHINI AND COD LASAGNA

Method: easy   Preparation time: 30 min
Cooking time: 20 min

– ✳ –

Serves 6

8 medium-sized zucchini

Slab of cod (1 lb. 5 oz)

6 anchovy fillets in oil

1 1/3 cups Parmesan

1 clove garlic

2 1/4 cups strong

court bouillon

Salt and pepper

1 attractive gratin dish

For the béchamel:

4 tablespoons

all-purpose flour

1/3 stick unsalted butter

2 1/4 cups mixed half milk,

half court bouillon

Salt and pepper

– ✳ –

Poach the cod in the barely simmering court bouillon for 8 min then leave to cool.

Filter the court bouillon and skin, bone and shred the fish.

Heat the milk and court bouillon mixture (2 1/8 cups each).

To make the béchamel, melt the butter in a saucepan, add the flour and stir with a wooden spoon. When the mixture starts to bubble, remove from the heat and gradually blend in the milk, stirring constantly. Return to the heat still stirring and mix in the anchovies and pepper.

Grate the Parmesan. Wash and dry the zucchini and slice thinly lengthwise.

Butter a gratin dish, rub with garlic, then fill with alternating layers of zucchini, shredded cod, béchamel and a sprinkling of parmesan until all the ingredients have been used up finishing with a layer of zucchini sprinkled with Parmesan. Cook in a very hot oven at 450-475°F for 15 to 20 min.

This is a vegetarian alternative to traditional lasagna.

$\mathcal{G}$ RATIN OF SWISS CHARD WITH ANCHOVIES

Method: quite easy   Preparation time: 30 min
Cooking time: 30 min

— ✳ —

Serves 8-10

2 plump, firm stalks

Swiss chard

10 salted anchovies

1 minced onion

1 garlic clove

3 egg yolks

1 good cup light cream

1 1/2 cups poultry broth

2 tablespoons olive oil

Drizzle vinegar

Pepper

For the chard:

2 lemons

1 tablespoon

all purpose flour

1 tablespoon olive oil

— ✳ —

Clean the chard carefully removing any tough outer threads then immerse in a basin of cold water with the juice of one lemon.

In a bowl, mix 1 tablespoon of flour with the juice of the remaining lemon and the olive oil. Add to a large saucepan of boiling water, beating constantly. Plunge in the chard and cook until tender. Drain and dice.

Rinse and bone the anchovies. Heat the olive oil in a casserole dish and blend the anchovies with the chopped onions. Sprinkle with 2 tablespoons of flour, mix well and add the garlic. Still stirring, pour on the hot broth then add the cream and chard. Cook for 10 min. Now beat the egg yolks into an omelet, add a drizzle of vinegar, beat into the casserole dish and cook in a very low oven for 5 min.

Transfer to an attractive gratin dish, garnish with anchovies and oven-broil for a few moments.

You will need to rinse your hands in lemon juice after cleaning the chard because it stains the skin black. Choose fleshy chard with firm, broad creamy white stalks.

SERVE WITH:
A rosé or white Côtes de Provence.

$\mathcal{F}$RIED POLENTA SPECIALLY FOR MY FRIEND HERVÉ

*Method: easy   Preparation time: 5 min
Cooking time: 15 min*

- ❋ -

Serves 4

**1 good cup fine-grained
maize semolina**

3 tablespoons olive oil

1/3 stick butter

1 piece mozzarella

2 1/4 cups milk

2 1/4 cups broth

2 garlic cloves (minced)

1 bunch basil

Salt and pepper

- ❋ -

In a skillet, heat a tablespoon of olive oil with the butter. Add the chopped garlic, snipped basil and sprinkle in the semolina. Cook for 5 min stirring constantly with a wooden spoon. Season and gradually add the boiling water (or broth). When completely absorbed add the milk until that too has been completely absorbed. Smooth the surface of the polenta with a spatula, cover with mozzarella slices, drizzle with olive oil and broil in the oven.
Serve piping hot straight from the skillet.

Hervé Amiard, my favorite photographer, is particularly fond of this dish which I often serve with a fricassee of rabbit or kid.

SERVE WITH:
A well balanced white Domaine de la Royère Côtes du Luberon.

MEAT

$\mathcal{L}$AMB CHARLOTTE WITH EGGPLANTS

*Method: quite hard   Preparation time: 30 min the day before
Cooking time: 1 hour*

— ✳ —

Serves 6
Leg of lamb
(about 3 lb. 4 oz,
cut into small dice)
6-7 long, firm eggplants
1/4 cup minced onions
1/2 teaspoon minced garlic
4-5 tablespoons
all purpose flour
1/3 cup tomato *concassé*
(see p. 108)
BLEND OF THE FOLLOWING
SPICES:
2 teaspoons cumin powder
1 teaspoon ground
coriander
1 teaspoon cinnamon
1/2 teaspoon
powdered ginger
1 sprig snipped tarragon
Fresh thyme
1 small chili
1 small piece candied ginger
1 quart + 3 cups white wine
Blanched zest 1 orange
and 1 lime
3/8 cup honey
Salt and pepper
Olive oil
Basil

— ✳ —

Heat the olive oil in a high-sided skillet. Sear the onions and meat, sprinkle with a pinch of flour and pour in the white wine.

Add the spices, chopped zest of orange and lime, honey, concassé of tomatoes and finally the chopped garlic.

Adjust the seasoning, cook for 45 min to 1 hour until the meat is tender and thoroughly cooked. Then remove the meat and reduce the sauce by three-quarters.

Meanwhile, slice the eggplants lengthwise and brush all over with olive oil.

Place under the broiler until golden brown then drain any excess fat on a piece of kitchen towel. Line the base of a deep cake pan with a ring of eggplant slices, cover with the meat followed by another ring of tightly, overlapping eggplant slices. Put a plate on top and weight it heavily.

Leave to chill overnight.

Just before dinner, place in a double boiler and warm over a low heat for 30 min. Turn out onto an attractive serving dish, decorate the center with basil and coarsely chopped tomatoes and coat with sauce.

This has been my favorite dish for some years now, ever since it was created quite by accident one Easter due to an error in the recipe. Thanks to a masterful blend of spices full of eastern promise, it transforms the rather too virile tian d'agneau (lamb quiche) into this delicate lamb charlotte with eggplants.

SERVE WITH:
A tannic, nicely aged red Hermitage.

STEWED KID WITH SPRING VEGETABLES

*Method: quite easy   Preparation time: 30 min
Cooking time: 45 min*

— ✳ —

Serves 6

**3 lb. joint of kid
(shoulder, chop, half leg)
on the bone, chopped
into even pieces**

4 peeled tomatoes

1/3 stick unsalted butter

10 small potatoes

1/2 cup oil

10 carrots with greens

6 small turnips with greens

Handful fresh, shelled peas

**Handful fresh, stripped
green beans**

Handful snow peas

**Handful cooked and peeled
broad beans**

6 small onions

3 garlic cloves

Pinch sugar

**2 tablespoons
all purpose flour**

1 bouquet garni

1/5 cup bacon (diced)

1 large onion (minced)

2 carrots

Fresh chervil

Salt and pepper

— ✳ —

Peel all the vegetables.

Next, heat the oil and butter in a cast-iron casserole dish and fry the pieces of meat until brown all over. Add the large onion, minced garlic, two sliced carrots and salt and pepper. When the meat is nicely sautéed, remove excess grease and sprinkle with sugar. Mix thoroughly and cook until slightly soft and sticky. Now sprinkle with flour, stir and leave to brown lightly.

Fill the dish with sufficient water to cover, add the fresh, peeled tomatoes and the bouquet garni. Bring to a boil, cover and cook in a gentle oven for 40-45 min. Then take out, remove the largest bones and set aside.

Glaze the baby onions in a skillet with a knob of butter then set aside. Brown the diced bacon and set that aside too.

Cook the vegetables one after the other in a small saucepan of boiling salted water. Take out when half cooked, drain and set aside. Coat the potatoes in oil and sauté in the skillet for 5 min.

Spoon off any surface fat from the sauce the meat was cooked in. Place over a low heat then add the meat, potatoes, onions, diced bacon, carrots and turnips and bring back to a boil. Just before serving, add the green beans, snow peas, peas and broad beans.

Serve in the casserole dish decorated with fresh chervil.

SERVE WITH:
**A mature Pauillac or Médoc or a distinctively rounded
Domaine de la Citadelle Côtes du Lubéron.**

$\mathcal{F}$RICASSÉ OF BABY RABBIT WITH SPLIT OLIVES

Method: quite easy   Preparation time: 10 min
Cooking time: 1 hour 15 min

— ✳ —

Serves 6

1 rabbit (4 lb. 6 oz)

or two baby rabbits

cut into 12 pieces

2/3 cup tomato concassé

1 large shredded onion

1 bunch thyme

and rosemary

6 garlic cloves

Bare 1/4 cup olive oil

1 quart red wine

(Côtes du Lubéron)

1 1/4 cups small green

olives (split)

1 quart poultry broth

(or bouillon cube)

1 ounce cultivated

mushrooms

2/3 cup diced bacon

4-5 tablespoons

all-purpose flour

1 tablespoon currant jelly

Salt and pepper

— ✳ —

In a deep-sided skillet, toss the shredded onion in some warmed olive oil until nicely golden. Remove from the skillet and set aside.

In the same oil, brown the diced bacon and sliced mushrooms sprinkled with lemon juice. Set that aside too.

Still using the same oil, fry the pieces of rabbit until brown all over. Sprinkle with flour, stirring well with a wooden spoon. Add the tomato concassé, minced garlic, herbs, salt and pepper. Pour on the red wine and the poultry broth. Stir well, cover and cook for around 35 min.

Add the onions, diced bacon and mushrooms and cook for a further 10 min. Then add the olives and currant jelly.

Check that the meat is thoroughly cooked, then remove from the skillet and reduce the sauce for 10 min.

Serve in a casserole dish with a slice of crispy golden bread fried in olive oil.

Delicious with fried polenta.

SERVE WITH:
A red Domaine de la Royère Côtes du Lubéron with a delicately tannic bouquet. The wine should be at room temperature.

*R*OAST PORK WITH SAGE

Method: easy   Preparation time: 5 min
Cooking time: 1hour 30 min the day before,
30 min on the day

— ✳ —

Serves 6

1 loin boned pork

1 large bunch sage

10 garlic cloves in their skin

1/2 stick unsalted butter

3 tablespoons sunflower oil

salt and pepper

— ✳ —

Place the boned loin of pork on a cookie sheet with the bones alongside. Add the garlic cloves in their skins and scatter sage leaves over the top. Butter the meat, season and baste with oil.

Preheat the oven to 225°F and bake for 1 hour 30 min, basting every 20 min. Then remove the meat from the oven, wrap in tin foil and leave to cool.

The next day, preheat the oven to 400°F and roast the pork in its juices for around 25 – 30 min depending on weight.

The long cooking time in a very low oven keeps the meat beautifully moist.

SERVE WITH:
A light, fruity red Côtes du Rhône.

*S*UNDAY POULTRY STUFFED WITH FARMER'S CHEESE

Method: easy   Preparation time: 40 min
Cooking time: 1 hour

— ❋ —

Serves 12

1 free-range chicken

(4 lb. 6 oz) without giblets

and ask the butcher to free

the skin from the carcass

1 trussed guinea fowl

(without giblets)

2 pigeons (without giblets)

1 lb. grapes (Muscat)

1 onion

1/2 stick unsalted butter

Oil

Salt and pepper

FOR THE CHICKEN STUFFING:

1/3 stick unsalted butter

2 good tablespoons farmer's

cheese

1 bunch mixed herbs

(tarragon, chervil, cilantro)

FOR THE PIGEON STUFFING:

Pigeon livers and hearts

2 shallots

2 eggs

1 dash Armagnac

2 cups white breadcrumbs

(from a stale loaf)

Milk

6 juniper berries

Fine kitchen string

and trussing needle

— ❋ —

Chicken: mix the melted butter with the farmer's cheese then stir in the chopped herbs, salt and pepper. Using a decorating bag, pipe the mixture under the skin of the chicken.

Truss the chicken with fine kitchen string, carefully sewing up the extremities. Pat with knobs of butter and place inside the oiled broiling pan. Roast in a hot oven for 45 min, basting every now and then.

Guinea fowl: season, rub lightly with oil, pat with knobs of butter and place inside the oven after the chicken has been cooking for 10 min.

Pigeons: soak the breadcrumbs in the milk then squeeze out any excess. Chop up the hearts and livers and mix with the soaked bread, eggs, minced shallots, Armagnac, crushed juniper berries, salt and pepper. Stuff the pigeons with this mixture, then truss and cook in a casserole dish with oil and butter, turning them after 20 min.

Finishing touches: peel half the grapes and squeeze out the juice from the remaining grapes. Peel and shred the onion, sauté until golden in the casserole dish then add the peeled grapes. Take the guinea fowl out of the oven, place it in the casserole dish, add the grape juice, salt, pepper and cook for a further 5 min. Bring the poultry to the table on a large dish surrounded by potatoes. Serve the sauces separately.

SERVE WITH:
A virile Clape Cornas – a wine worth waiting for.

CRISPY PIGEON WITH SPICY HONEY

*Method: hard   Preparation time: 5 min the day before + 1 hour
Cooking time: 20 min*

- ✳ -

Serves 8

**4 boned pigeons
(about 1 lb. each)**

**1 1/3 cups cultivated
mushrooms (washed,
dried and diced)**

4 red onions (shredded)

3/4 cup oak honey

**1 packet ready-made
phyllo pastry**

1/2 cup cider vinegar

1 tablespoon ginger

3 minced garlic cloves

**1 lb. tub goose fat
(2 1/2 cups)**

1 sprig mint

1 sprig fresh thyme

Coarse sea salt

1 1/2 sticks unsalted butter

FOR THE PIGEON BROTH:

2 carrots

1 rib celery

1 onion

**Broken carcasses of
4 pigeons**

2 1/4 cups white wine

1 bouquet garni

Salt and pepper

- ✳ -

To prepare the pigeon broth: brown the pigeon carcasses with the chopped onion. Add the honey, carrots and celery then pour in the white wine and cider vinegar. Add the bouquet garni, salt and pepper and simmer over a low heat for 30 min. Now strain and set aside.

To prepare the glazed pigeon legs: the day before, sprinkle the legs with a tablespoon of coarse sea salt, fresh thyme and pepper. Chill overnight. The following day, rinse well and place in a cast-iron casserole dish with 2 cups goose fat. Cook for 1 hour until soft and slightly sticky and set aside.

To prepare the glazed onions: sauté the shredded red onions vigorously in a tablespoon of fat. Sprinkle with a dash of vinegar and a teaspoon of ginger and add a tablespoon of honey. Allow the liquid to evaporate and set aside. Sauté the mushrooms in the skillet then add the chopped garlic, salt and pepper. Set that aside too.

To prepare the filleted breasts: sear the skin in a tablespoon of fat and set aside.

Making-up: line a porcelain or glass pie plate with overlapping sheets of phyllo pastry leaving a wide border. Spread with a layer of mushrooms, top with the pigeon breasts, cover with the glazed onions and the snipped mint leaves adding a pinch of cinnamon. Join the edges of pastry with a cocktail stick, cover with a sheet of tin foil and set aside. When you are ready to serve, bake for 16 min at 425°F so that the flesh remains pink and underdone.

Meanwhile, reduce the broth and beat in the butter; reheat the legs for 10 min in the oven. Serve on mixed leaves.

$\mathcal{M}$ACARONI GRATIN WITH CALF SWEET-BREADS AND FOIE GRAS

Method: quite hard   Preparation time: 1 hour
Cooking time: 6 min for the sweetbreads + 10 min in the oven

– * –

Serves 6

1 packet long macaroni

6 small slices raw
duck's liver

2 calves' sweetbreads

Drizzle vinegar

1 glass Madeira wine
(bare 1 cup)

For the stuffing:

7 ounces veal filet
(filet mignon)

1 egg white

4 tablespoons crème fraîche

1 pinch allspice

1 teaspoon butter

Salt and pepper

FOR THE COURT BOUILLON:

1 onion

1/2 leek

1 bay leaf

Coarse sea salt

Pepper corns

1/2 carrot

6 small, rounded molds

– * –

Soak the sweetbreads in water with a dash of vinegar for 30 min removing any tough outer membrane. Make a court bouillon with the onion, half a leek, bay leaf, coarse sea salt, three pepper corns and half a carrot. Plunge the sweetbreads into the court bouillon and cook for 5-6 min over a low heat. Remove from the heat and leave to cool.

Cook the macaroni 'al dente' in a large pan of boiling water then strain. Finish cleaning the sweetbreads which should be perfectly smooth.

To prepare the stuffing: mince the veal fillet, place in a mixing bowl over ice, add the egg white and mix well. Season, add the allspice and cream then mix well with a spatula to give the mousse a light consistency. Slice the sweetbreads into fairly slim escalopes, fry in a skillet with a teaspoon of butter and set aside.

Making-up: brush six small rounded molds with butter and line with one length of macaroni in a spiral. Fill with a layer of stuffing, followed by a layer of sweetbreads and another layer of stuffing.

Approximately 10 min before serving, place the molds in a large roasting pan filled with water so that the molds are 2/3 submerged. Cook in a moderate oven at 350°F then remove and turn out.

Fry the slices of raw duck liver vigorously then de-glaze the skillet with a small glass of Madeira wine. Place a slice in the center of each gratin and coat with the cooking juices.

SERVE WITH:
A full-bodied, toasty Puligny-Montrachet Côte de Beaune
or a well structured white Côtes du Rhône Nord Condrieu
with a floral, honeyed bouquet.

$\mathcal{T}$ERRINE OF BABY RABBIT
WITH RED AND GREEN CABBAGE

Method: quite hard   Preparation time: 1 hour
Cooking time: 1 hour 45 min

— ❋ —

Serves around 10

2 small boned rabbits cut
into 20 pieces

1 piece neck of pork (1 lb.)

1 green cabbage

1 red cabbage

1 pork caul casing

6 eggs

1 tablespoon cognac

1 pinch allspice

Salt and pepper

For the marinade:

4 1/2 cups red wine

(Côtes du Lubéron)

1 tablespoon cognac

1 tablespoon olive oil

2 large onions stuck
with a clove

3 garlic cloves

2-3 onions

3 juniper berries

Peel of 1 orange

1 bouquet garni

— ❋ —

Prepare the marinade the day before. Shred the onions and peel the garlic cloves, mix with the red wine, olive oil and cognac and pour over the pieces of rabbit. Add the remaining marinade ingredients and chill for 24 hours.

On the day, prepare the stuffing: blanch the neck of pork for a few min, drain, pat dry and chop together with the flesh of the rabbit legs. Add the onions, garlic and the marinade. Mix well, add the eggs, spices and cognac, stir again and chill for 1 hour.

Heat 1 tablespoon of olive oil in a skillet then fry the liver and saddle of rabbit just enough to sear.

Strip and wash the cabbages and cook the separated leaves in boiling salted water. Cool in cold water, drain and dry on a tea towel. Remove any tough stalks.

Soak the caul casing in cold water, rinse and dry well.

Making-up: line a rectangular terrine dish with the caul casing. Then fill with a layer of green cabbage, red cabbage, a little of the stuffing, a few red and green cabbage leaves, the saddle of rabbit cut into escalopes, the minced livers, another layer of stuffing and finally another layer of cabbage leaves. Now fold over the caul casing.

Place the terrine dish in a roasting pan filled with 3-4 inches boiling water and cook at 325°F for 1 hour 45 min. Leave to cool then cover with a plate and put a 2 lb. weight on top.

I like to serve this terrine with fruit and vegetable jam and a few cherries in homemade vinegar (see p. 108).

SERVE WITH:
An intensely aromatic Château de Mille Blanc Côtes du Lubéron.

74

FISH

*M*EDITERRANEAN SEA BASS
IN A SALT CRUST

Method: easy   Preparation: 20 min + 1 hour rest time
Cooking time: 25 min

– ✳ –

Serves 6

1 plump sea bass

(about 3 lb. 4 oz)

4 cups unrefined sea salt

1/2 cup best quality

unrefined sea salt

2 1/4 cups all-purpose flour

2/3 cup water

2 egg whites

1 bunch fresh rosemary

Pepper

– ✳ –

Ask your fishmonger to clean and trim the gills of the sea bass leaving the scales. Keep in the refrigerator until needed.

Snip the sprigs of rosemary into tiny pieces setting aside 1 tablespoon. Season the belly of the sea bass with the remaining snipped rosemary and return to the refrigerator.

In a large mixing bowl, mix the unrefined and pure sea salt, the flour, egg whites and the tablespoon of snipped rosemary. Gradually add enough water to form a dough, chill for 1 hour then roll out and use to line the base of an oven-proof dish. Place the sea bass inside, pepper and cover with another layer of salt crust so that the fish is completely encased.

Cook at 400°F for 25 min.

Remove the fish by breaking open the salt crust. Carve the sea bass and serve with a knob of rosemary flavored butter.

SERVE WITH:
A refreshing, lively white Bellet from the Alpes Maritimes.

$\mathcal{M}$ARINADE OF RED MULLET

Method: quite hard   Preparation time: 30 min to fillet
Cooking time: 5 min

– ✳ –

Serves 6

12 filleted red mullets

de-boned with tweezers

3 garlic cloves

2 shallots

1/2 small chili

1 bay leaf

1 sprig thyme

1/2 tablespoon

ground ginger

Bare 1 cup vinegar

1 cup dry white wine

1/2 tablespoon

coriander seeds

1/4 cup olive oil

Salt and pepper

– ✳ –

Heat the oil in a large non-stick skillet then fry the snipped shallots and minced garlic until lightly golden. Sauté the red mullet with its skin for 2 min, sprinkle with vinegar, season and transfer to a platter. Pour the white wine plus the remaining condiments into the skillet, reduce the juices for 2 min and pour onto the fillets.
Serve warm or cold.

SERVE WITH:
A white Cassis.

$\mathcal{S}$ARDINE GRATIN WITH GARDEN HERBS

Method: easy   Preparation time: 15 min
Cooking time: 15 min

— ✳ —

Serves 6

24 small de-scaled sardines,

heads off

1 lb. spinach

1 bunch sorrel

1/3 cup tomato *concassé*

(see p. 108)

1 bunch rosemary

2 tablespoons roasted

pine nuts

2 tablespoons olive oil

Salt and pepper

— ✳ —

Wash the spinach and sorrel, remove the stalks and blanche. Arrange the 12 filleted sardines on a cookie tray. Cover the remaining sardines, season and set aside in the refrigerator. To prepare the stuffing: heat some oil in a saucepan, add the minced garlic, blanched spinach and the tomato *concassé*. Leave to stew for 5 min then add the sorrel and roasted pine nuts. Chop the stuffing coarsely with a knife then place two tablespoons on the opened-out sardines. Cover with a second sardine, season, drizzle with olive oil and prick with a sprig of rosemary. Bake in the oven at 450°F for 5 min.

These sardines are delicious barbecued on a summer evening.

SERVE WITH:
A young Clairette de Languedoc.

CREAMY SCALLOP SOUP

Method: quite hard   Preparation time: 35 min
Cooking time: 20 min

- ✳ -

Serves 6

12 scallops

2 carrots

1/2 onion

2 ribs celery

2 turnips

1 fennel bulb

1 large zucchini

4 tablespoons olive oil

Peel of 1 orange

1 bay leaf

Saffron

4 egg yolks

2 tablespoons heavy cream

FOR THE ROUILLE:

4 garlic cloves

1 small, red Spanish chili

1 tablespoon breadcrumbs

pre-soaked in milk and

strained

1 egg yolk

1 cup olive oil

Salt and Cayenne pepper

- ✳ -

Start by making the rouille, a mayonnaise flavored with garlic, chili and fish broth. Grind the four garlic cloves in a mortar (or in the blender) along with the red chili and the drained breadcrumbs. Transfer to a mixing bowl, add an egg yolk, salt and cayenne pepper and gradually work up into a mayonnaise with half a glass of olive oil. Chill until needed.

Shred the onion, carrots, ribs of celery, turnips and fennel into matchstick size strips. Chop the washed (but not peeled) zucchini into slim round slices. Heat 4 tablespoons olive oil in a large saucepan and toss in all the vegetables except for the zucchini. Add the orange peel, a pinch of coarse salt and some pepper. Sweat over a low heat for 5 min then add the zucchini and the scallops. Cook for 7 min, remove from the heat and strain retaining the broth.

When you are ready to serve, thicken the broth by adding 4 egg yolks combined with 4 tablespoons of the *rouille* and 2 tablespoons of heavy cream. Return to a low heat until the broth has taken on the consistency of custard.

Arrange the vegetables and scallops in the center of the soup dish then cover with the thickened broth. Serve the *rouille* to one side.

SERVE WITH:
A white Graves, preferably a Pessac-Léognan.

SAUTÉED TELLINAS

*Method: quite easy   Preparation time: 15 min after cleaning
Cooking time: 5 min*

— ✳ —

Serves 6

**2 lb. 3 oz cleaned tellinas
(or other small shellfish)**

2 garlic cloves (minced)

1/2 cup olive oil

1 bunch parsley (chopped)

Drizzle lemon juice

Salt and pepper

— ✳ —

Cleaning tellinas is by far the hardest part of this recipe. Soak them for several hours in sea water then scrub vigorously under the tap to remove all the sand. Now heat a skillet until very hot, toss in the tellinas, wait for 3 min and cover. Add garlic, olive oil, salt, pepper, a drizzle of lemon juice and sprinkle with minced parsley just before serving. Delicious, warm or cold.

Tellinas live all year round in the sandy beaches of the Carmague in southern France but they are at their most delicious in summer. For a slightly different flavor, strain after cooking to remove the juices and blend carefully with a light aïol (garlic mayonnaise). Where tellinas are not available you can of course substitute other small shellfish.

SERVE WITH:
A lively Picpoul de Pinet from the Hérault region in France.

SKEWERS OF SMALL GRAY SNAILS WITH AÏOLI

Method: quite easy   Preparation time: 30 min
Cooking time: 15 min

— ✳ —

Serves 8-10

1 slice squash

Nutmeg

4 cups small gray snails

6 carrots

1/2 cauliflower

6 red skinned potatoes

6 broccoli spears

41/2 cups strong

vegetable broth

Peel of 1 orange

3 pepper corns

Salt

For the aïoli:

1/2 head peeled

and cored garlic

2 egg yolks

2 1/4 cups cold

pressed olive oil from

the first pressing

Dash lemon juice

— ✳ —

Peel all the vegetables. Separate the half cauliflower and broccoli into little flowerets, dice the slice of squash, chop the carrots into little segments and cut the potatoes into round slices. Steam the cauliflower, broccoli, squash and potatoes separately. Cook the carrots in boiling water.

To make the aïoli: grind the garlic in a mortar blending in the eggs, olive oil, salt, pepper and a dash of lemon juice.

Rinse the snails. Heat the vegetable broth, add the orange peel, pepper corns and snails and simmer for 5 min. Strain then thread the snails onto the skewers followed by the vegetables, another snail and so on.

Serve warm with the aïoli.

This amusing dish is an alternative to the aioli traditionally served on Christmas Eve in Provence with the 'souper maigre' (lean supper) based on cod.

SERVE WITH:
A white Coteaux du Languedoc.

DESSERTS

*P*EACH SOUP WITH LEMON VERBENA

*Method: easy   Preparation time: 15 min the day before
Cooking time: 30 min for the syrup*

— ✳ —

Serve 6

2 quarts ripe white peaches

1 cup lemon juice

4 1/2 cups syrup made

with 4 1/2 cups water

and 2 1/4 cups sugar

1 bunch lemon verbena

plus a few leaves fresh

lemon verbena

— ✳ —

Boil the water and sugar for about 30 min, add the verbena and leave to infuse (there should be 41/2 cups water left).

Peel the peaches by soaking in boiling water for 2 min. Remove the pits and set half the peaches aside.

Mix the remaining peaches with the cooled syrup, add the lemon juice and chill. On the day, slice the peaches you set aside and add to the soup.

Serve deliciously chilled, decorated with leaves of fresh verbena.

SERVE WITH:
A peach wine.

STRAWBERRY TART

*Method: easy   Preparation time: 30 min
Cooking time: 20 min*

− ✳ −

Serves 6

7 oz sweet pie crust

1 cup French vanilla cream

1 1/2 cups strawberries

1 tablespoon icing sugar

Fresh mint

1 11-inch loose-based

quiche pan

− ✳ −

Line a loose-based quiche pan with 1/2 inch of sweet pie crust and bake for 20 min at 350°F.

When cool, spread with a layer of French vanilla cream and the de-stalked strawberries. Dust with icing sugar and decorate with fresh mint leaves.

Always wash the strawberries before removing the stalks, handling as delicately as possible.

RED BERRY SOUP

*Method: very easy   Preparation time: 10 min
Cooking time: 35 min the day before*

− ✳ −

Serves 8-10

2 1/2 quarts raspberries

2 1/4 cups sugar

2 1/4 cups water

1 cup lemon juice

fresh mint

− ✳ −

Make the syrup first by boiling the water and sugar for 30 min then leave to cool.

The next day, mash half the strawberries and pass through a strainer to remove the seeds. Mix with the syrup and lemon.

Pour into individual goblets and add the remaining fruit. Decorate with mint leaves.

This heavenly summer soup may be made with strawberries, raspberries or currants depending on the season

SERVE WITH:
A Muscat de Rivesaltes with a lemony, floral bouquet.

94

WARM FRUITS OF THE ORCHARD PIE

Method: easy   Preparation: 30 min
Cooking time: 40 min

– ✸ –

Serves 6

2 1/2 quarts pitted cherries

10 apricots

15 fresh almonds

1 egg

2 tablespoons

superfine sugar

1 9-inch pie plate

FOR THE SWEET PIE CRUST:

1 1/3 cups all-purpose flour

2/3 stick unsalted butter

1 egg yolk

1 teaspoon superfine sugar

Bare 1 cup water

Pinch salt

FOR THE CREAM:

1/2 cup granulated sugar

4 1/2 tablespoons

all purpose flour

4 tablespoons heavy cream

1 1/2 tablespoons soft

unsalted butter

1 whole egg

– ✸ –

To make the sweet pie crust (pâte sablée): place the flour in a mixing bowl with the cold butter cut into small pieces, the sugar, salt and egg yolk. Work the butter and egg into the dry ingredients until the mixture has a sandy texture then add enough water to form a compact dough. Chill. Pit the cherries and apricots and set aside.

To make the cream: stirring delicately, combine the soft butter with the sugar and the sifted flour. Leave at room temperature for 15 min then add the beaten egg.

Carefully line a buttered and floured pie plate with the crust, leaving a wide overhanging border. Prick with a fork, spread with fruit, cover with cream then fold and gently press down the edges of the crust. Brush with beaten egg, bake at 350-375°F then dust with sugar, prick with almonds and brown under the broiler for 3 to 4 min.

SERVE WITH:
A vintage Rivesaltes with a bouquet of honey and quince.

96

$\mathcal{C}$LAFOUTIS (BATTER PUDDING) WITH HOMEGROWN CHERRIES

*Method: easy   Preparation time: 30 min
Cooking time: 30-40 min*

‒ ❋ ‒

Serves 6

**2 1/2 quarts homegrown
cherries**

**1 1/2 tablespoons soft
unsalted butter**

4 whole eggs

4 tablespoons sugar

FOR THE BATTER:

Bare 1 cup sugar

**Good 1/2 cup
all-purpose flour**

2/3 cup heavy cream

4 eggs

‒ ❋ ‒

First, steep the cherries in a bowl with the sugar and butter.
To make the batter: whiten the eggs and sugar in a blender then
add the flour followed by the cream.
Pour the fruits into an oven-proof dish, cover with the batter
and bake at 350-375°F for 30 to 40 min.
Serve warm.

$\mathcal{F}$RESH FIGS TOPPED WITH HONEYED MOUSSE

‒ ❋ ‒

Serves 6

1 1/3 quarts fresh figs

**1/4 cup light
whipping cream**

**3 1/2 tablespoons
lavender honey**

Bare 1 cup Grand Marnier)

Pretty glass bowl to serve

‒ ❋ ‒

Method: very easy   Preparation time: 10 min

Wash, dry and slice the figs. Beat the cream with a whisk until
light and frothy then add the honey and Grand Marnier.
Place the figs in a pretty glass bowl, cover with the honeyed
mousse and chill for at least one hour.

SERVE WITH:

A Muscat Beaumes-de-Venise such as a delicious Castaud Maurin.

*C*HERRY NOUGAT

Method: easy
Preparation time: 30 min several hours in advance

— ❋ —

Serves 6

2 lb. 3 oz strained

farmer's cheese

2 3/4 cups heavy

crème fraîche

1 1/3 cups candied cherries

1 good cup almonds

1 good cup hazelnuts

1/2 cup acacia honey

1 tablespoon kirsch

3 envelopes gelatin

1 cake pan with

sloping sides

— ❋ —

Strain the farmer's cheese and soften the gelatin in a little cold water. Chop the almonds and hazelnuts in the food processor. Heat the honey in a saucepan, add the gelatin and leave to dissolve. In a mixing bowl, combine the farmer's cheese with the honey and gelatin, chopped cherries, dried fruit and kirsch. Stir well. Beat the cream until stiff and fold carefully into the cheese mixture. Pour into a mold and chill for at least 3 hours. Decorate with cherry halves and serve with a coulis of cherries.

In France, I make this nougat with bigarreaux *(whiteheart) cherries grown in the region around Gordes and then candied in the traditional manner by a local confectioner called 'Cigalette'*

SERVE WITH:
A smooth Rasteau fragrant with notes of soft cooked fruits.

$\mathcal{C}$HEESECAKE MADE WITH FARMER'S GOATS CHEESE AND FLAVORED WITH LEMON BALM AND CITRONELLA

Method: easy   Preparation time: 15 min
Cooking time: 50 min

— ✳ —

Serves 6

1 1/3 cups farmer's
goats cheese
1 1/2 cups crème fraîche
2/3 cup superfine sugar
1/2 melted butter
4 eggs
Rind of 2 lemons
1 bunch lemon balm
and citronella
1 glazed earthenware dish

— ✳ —

Grate the lemon rind. Separate the eggs and beat the yolks in a bowl with the sugar until white and creamy. Add the cheese, crème fraiche, lemon rind and melted butter.

Snip the lemon balm. Beat the egg whites until stiff, fold delicately into the cheese mixture and add the lemon balm. Turn into the buttered dish and bake in a low oven (325°F) for 50 min. Serve warm or cold with fig jam and chopped fresh almonds.

SERVE WITH:
A medium dry Anjou.

$\mathcal{B}$LACK NOUGAT

Method: quite hard   Preparation time: 15 min, 24 hours in advance
Cooking time: 20-30 min

— ✳ —

Serves 12

2 3/4 cups honey
1 3/4 cups husked almonds
1 Sheet wax paper
1 homemade wooden frame

— ✳ —

Heat the honey over a low heat in a small, preferably copper saucepan. Bring to a boil stirring constantly. Add the husked almonds and boil for 5−6 min until the honey starts to caramelize. Now lay a wooden frame on a board, fill it with the honey, cover with wax paper and weight down.

Chill for 24 hours.

SERVE WITH:
A Vin Doux Naturel from the Vaucluse, such as a smooth Rasteau.

$\mathcal{T}$HIRTEEN DESSERTS IN A HONEY FLAVORED FARMER'S CHEESE LOG CAKE

Method: quite easy   Preparation time: 25 min

— ❋ —

Serves 8-10

3 1/3 cups farmer's sheep's cheese

Bare 3/4 cup candied fruit (melons, oranges, lemons, cherries)

1 1/2 sticks nougatine (store bought)

1 1/3 cups mixed nuts (almonds, hazelnuts, pine nuts, pistachios)

1 cup crème fraîche for whipping

Good 1/2 cup honey

3 1/2 envelopes gelatin

FOR THE TOPPING:

5/8 cup light cream

1 saucer of raspberry or strawberry coulis

Candied fruits

— ❋ —

Soften the gelatin in a little cold water. Warm the honey then combine with the gelatin and leave to cool.

Cut the candied fruit into little cubes, roughly chop the nuts, crush the nougatine. In a cold mixing bowl, whip the crème fraîche until stiff. Then, in a separate mixing bowl, mash the farmer's cheese with a fork and combine with the nuts, candied fruit and nougatine. Add the honey, stir and delicately fold in the whipped cream. Chill until the mixture starts to set.

Now transfer onto a large sheet of plastic wrap and roll into a fat sausage. Wrap tightly in the plastic wrap and chill once again. When the log cake is quite firm, remove the plastic wrap, beat the whipping cream until stiff and spread with a fork. Decorate with cherries and pieces of candied fruit and serve with a coulis.

This creamy log cake is inspired by the 13 desserts traditionally served at Christmas time in Provence.

SERVE WITH:
A Muscat Beaumes-de-Venise reminiscent of roses.

$\mathcal{H}$OME-MADE *CALISSON*
WITH CARDAMOM ICE-CREAM

Method: quite easy   Preparation time: 30 min
Cooking time: 20 min

— ✳ —

Serves 8-10

FOR THE *CALISSON*:

1 1/3 cups sugar

2 cups ground almonds

5/8 cup apricot jam

2 sheets Holy

Communion wafer

(if available)

3/4 cup icing sugar

1 egg white

FOR THE ICE CREAM:

2 1/4 cups milk

1/3 cup light cream

1/2 cup granulated sugar

4 egg yolks

10 lightly crushed

cardamom seeds

Good tablespoon

acacia honey

— ✳ —

To make the *calisson*, pour the sugar, ground almonds and jam into a heavy-based saucepan. Stir over a low heat to obtain a dry paste then turn into a mold previously lined with Holy Communion wafer (optional).

Beat the icing sugar with the egg white and pour onto the *calisson* mixture. Dry in a very low oven (275°F) for 10 min and leave to cool.

To make the ice cream: blend the egg yolks and sugar until light and creamy, then stir in the honey. Bring the milk and cream to a boil, add the crushed cardamom seeds and mix with the previous mixture. Leave to steep for at least 30 min. When cool, strain and place in the ice cream maker.

Serve spoonfuls of *calisson* with the ice cream.

This is a much larger version of the traditional *calisson*, a lozenge-shaped sweet made of marzipan.

SERVE WITH:
A fortified wine from the Domaine des Bastides.

——— - ✳ - ———

The recipes given here are invaluable for anyone
with a serious interest in Provençale and indeed French cuisine.

$\mathscr{C}$HERRIES IN VINEGAR

Method: easy
Preparation time: 20 min
at least one month in advance
Cooking time: 10 min

Makes 1 quart jar of cherries

1 1/2 quarts whiteheart cherries (or other), 2 1/4 cups
wine vinegar, 1/4 cup turbinado sugar, 2 cloves, pinch of
pepper corns, 1 sprig tarragon, 1 garlic clove.
Wash and drain the cherries and snip off the
tip of the stalk (1/2 inch).
Gradually bring the vinegar to a boil, adding
the spices, brown sugar and garlic.
Place the cherries in the jar.
Pour on the warm vinegar and add
the tarragon. Close the jar and
eat one month later.
Cherries in vinegar are a delicious alternative
to gerkins when serving terrines.
If whiteheart cherries are not available, morel-
los will do equally well.

$\mathscr{C}$ONCASSÉ OF TOMATOES

Method: easy
Preparation time: 30 min
Cooking time: 1 hour

Makes 11 lb. concassé

6 1/2 lb. tomatoes, 1 head garlic, peeled and cored,
3 shallots, bare 1/2 cup olive oil, teaspoon sugar, 1 bunch
fresh thyme, 1 bunch snipped basil, salt and pepper
Peel the tomatoes by plunging in boiling
water for a few moments.

Remove the seeds and quarter.
Peel and mince the shallot then sauté in olive
oil in a braising pan. Add the tomatoes, minced garlic, thyme, snipped basil, sugar, salt
and pepper. Cover and stew for 30 min until
all the juice from the tomatoes has evapora-
ted. Cool and eat immediately
or freeze in trays. I use Roma or Italian tomatoes for this recipe which are not as juicy as
plum tomatoes and therefore
require less evaporation.

$\mathscr{W}$INTER FRUIT AND VEGETABLE JAM

Method: easy
Preparation time: 10 min
Cooking time: about 1 hour 30 min
Makes 2 lb. 2oz jam

1 small squash (11 oz), 2 quinces, 2 apples, 2 pears,
2 carrots, 1 rib celery, 1 organic lemon, 1 lime, peel of
1 orange, 4 1/2 cups cider vinegar, 2 1/4 cups turbinado
sugar, 2 tablespoons mustard seeds, 5 cloves, 1 cinnamon
stick, 2 tablespoons powdered ginger, 2 small chilis,
3 garlic cloves, 1 small ginger bulb
Bring the vinegar and brown sugar to a boil
in a large saucepan then add the spices.
Peel the fruit and vegetables
and cut into small pieces.
Cook the pieces of quince first, followed by
the carrots, squash, celery and lastly the
fruits. Cook over a low heat for at least
1 hour 30 min until soft and sticky.
Leave to cool and pour into individual jars.
Store in a cool place.

A NCHOÏADE
Method: very easy
Preparation time: 15 min
Cooking time: 10 min
Serves 6

One dozen salted anchovies, rinsed in running water
and soaked for 10 min to remove the salt,
bare 1/2 cup (best quality) olive oil,
1 teaspoon good vinegar,
1/2 cored garlic clove, freshly ground pepper
Wash and filet the anchovies.
Warm the olive oil then add the cored
garlic mashed with a fork, the anchovy filets
and the vinegar. Stir well and
do not allow to boil.
Add freshly ground pepper and leave to cool.

*S*ALT COD *BRANDADE*
Method: easy
Preparation time: 15 min
Cooking time: 25 min
Serves 10-12

One thick slab salt cod (2 lb. 2 oz),
2 1/4 cups olive oil, pinch allspice, 1 minced garlic clove,
pinch pepper, 4 1/2 cups milk,
2 1/4 cups light cream.
Soak the salt cod for 24 hours, changing
the water at frequent intervals.
Once the salt has been removed, heat the
milk in a large saucepan and plunge in the
cod. Bring to simmering point, strain, discard
the milk and bone the cod when cool.
Heat 2 tablespoons olive oil and the minced
garlic in a large skillet and cook for 2 min.
Add the cod, stir well and beat.
Heat the remaining olive oil and the cream

in two separate saucepans. Now, stirring
constantly, work into the cod mixture,
one tablespoon of each at a time until all the
oil and cream have been used up.
Sprinkle with allspice and pepper. Beat well
until the mixture turns quite thick and creamy.
Leave to cool and store in the refrigerator.

*T*APENADE
(BLACK OLIVE PASTE)
Method: easy
Preparation time: 30 min

Makes 2 lb. 2 oz paste
2 1/4 cups pitted black olives, 4 ounces anchovy filets,
3/4 cup capers, 2 tablespoons cognac,
4 garlic cloves (minced), bare 1 cup olive oil,
2 tablespoons mustard
Mash the olives, anchovies, caper
and garlic. Add the mustard, cognac
and work in the olive oil.
Season to taste.

*F*RITTER BATTER
Method: very easy
Preparation time: 5 min

Makes enough batter to prepare appetizers
for 8-10 people
1 1/3 cups all purpose flour (sifted),
bare 1/2 cup ice water, 2 tablespoons oil,
1 whole egg + 1 egg white.
Sift the flour into a large mixing bowl,
make a well in the middle and add the salt,
egg and oil. Stirring constantly, add the ice
water then whip the egg white
until it forms peaks. Fold delicately into
the batter and refrigerate until needed.

INDEX

Photographs shot at the Mas Tourteron or the Carré d'Herbes.

Mas Tourteron
chemin de Saint-Blaise, 84220 Gordes.
Tel: 04 90 72 00 16
Fax: 04 90 72 09 81

Le Carré d'Herbes
13, avenue des Quatre-Otages
84800 Isle-sur-la-Sorgue
Tel: 04 90 38 62 95

First published in France in 1999 by Editions du Chêne-Hachette Livre.
Copyright © 1999 Editions du Chêne-Hachette Livre. All rights reserved.

This edition published by Barnes & Noble, Inc., by arrangement with
Editions du Chêne-Hachette Livre.

2002 Barnes & Noble Books
M 10 9 8 7 6 5 4 3 2 1
ISBN 0-7607-3007-5

CREATIVE DIRECTION
Blandine Houdart

DESIGN
Sabine Houplain

LAYOUT
Jean-Claude Marguerite

TRANSLATED FROM THE FRENCH BY
Florence Brutton

Photoengraving: Euresys, Baisieux, France.
Binding and printing: Pollina, France. N° L85223